# LET'S PLAY SPORTS!
# Wrestling

by Jill Sherman

BLASTOFF!
2
READERS

BELLWETHER MEDIA • MINNEAPOLIS, MN

Note to Librarians, Teachers, and Parents:

**Blastoff! Readers** are carefully developed by literacy experts and combine standards-based content with developmentally appropriate text.

**Level 1** provides the most support through repetition of high-frequency words, light text, predictable sentence patterns, and strong visual support.

**Level 2** offers early readers a bit more challenge through varied simple sentences, increased text load, and less repetition of high-frequency words.

**Level 3** advances early-fluent readers toward fluency through increased text and concept load, less reliance on visuals, longer sentences, and more literary language.

**Level 4** builds reading stamina by providing more text per page, increased use of punctuation, greater variation in sentence patterns, and increasingly challenging vocabulary.

**Level 5** encourages children to move from "learning to read" to "reading to learn" by providing even more text, varied writing styles, and less familiar topics.

Whichever book is right for your reader, Blastoff! Readers are the perfect books to build confidence and encourage a love of reading that will last a lifetime!

This edition first published in 2020 by Bellwether Media, Inc.

No part of this publication may be reproduced in whole or in part without written permission of the publisher. For information regarding permission, write to Bellwether Media, Inc., Attention: Permissions Department, 6012 Blue Circle Drive, Minnetonka, MN 55343.

Library of Congress Cataloging-in-Publication Data

Title: Wrestling / by Jill Sherman.
Description: Minneapolis, MN : Bellwether Media, Inc., 2020. | Series: Blastoff! Readers : Let's Play Sports! | Includes bibliographical references and index. | Audience: Ages: 5-8. | Audience: Grades: K-3.
Identifiers: LCCN 2018058490 (print) | LCCN 2019004091 (ebook) | ISBN 9781618915443 (ebook) | ISBN 9781644870037 (hardcover : alk. paper)
Subjects: LCSH: Wrestling–Juvenile literature.
Classification: LCC GV1195.3 (ebook) | LCC GV1195.3 .S47 2020 (print) | DDC 796.812–dc23
LC record available at https://lccn.loc.gov/2018058490

Editor: Rebecca Sabelko     Designer: Andrea Schneider

Printed in the United States of America, North Mankato, MN.

# Table of Contents

# What Is Wrestling?

Wrestling is a sport in which two wrestlers use their strength and skill against one another.

Wrestlers try to control each other's movements. They try to **pin** their **opponents**.

pin

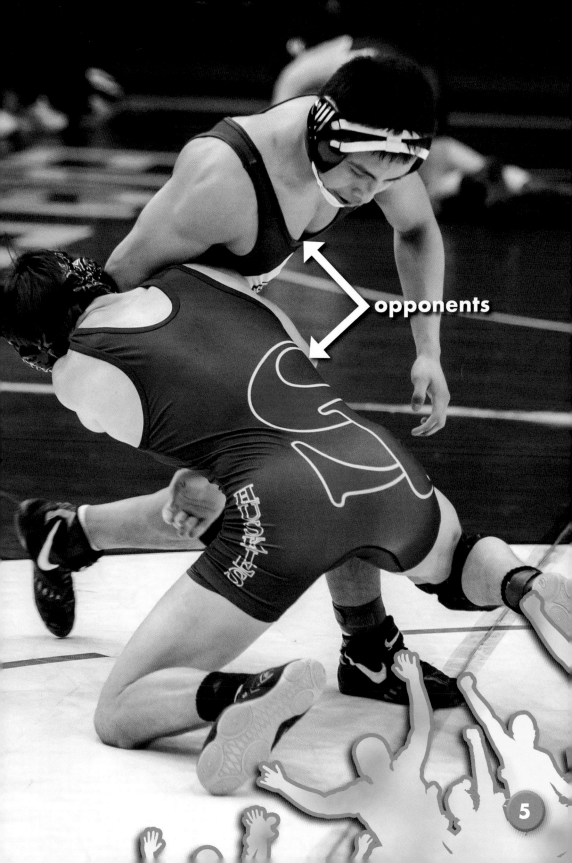

**opponents**

Wrestling is an individual and team sport. **Matches** take place on a mat.

- Iowa State University wrestling team

- United States Olympic Wrestling Team

- Accomplishments:

  - 3-time All-American college wrestler

  - 3-time USA Freestyle National Champion

  - World Champion in 1971

  - Olympic Gold Medalist in 1972

The sport is popular in many countries around the world. It is an **Olympic** sport!

# What Are the Rules for Wrestling?

Wrestlers are weighed before matches. This decides their **weight class**.

Wrestling matches are made up of three **periods**.

Wrestlers start matches in a **neutral** position. They stand facing one another.

neutral position

They try to bring one another
down to the mat. This is
called a **takedown**.

Wrestlers fight for control.
They try to pin their opponents.

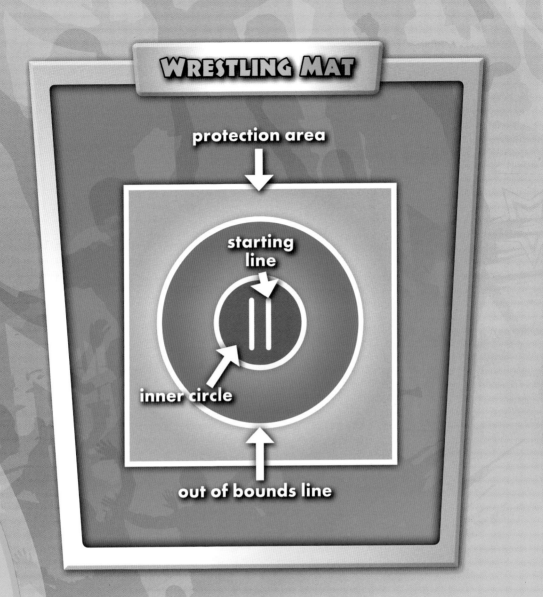

**WRESTLING MAT**

protection area

starting line

inner circle

out of bounds line

Pins win matches!
But not all matches
are won with a pin.

Some matches are won through points. Takedowns earn two points. Escaping **holds** earns one point.

Wrestlers who earn the most points win matches!

takedown

# Wrestling Gear

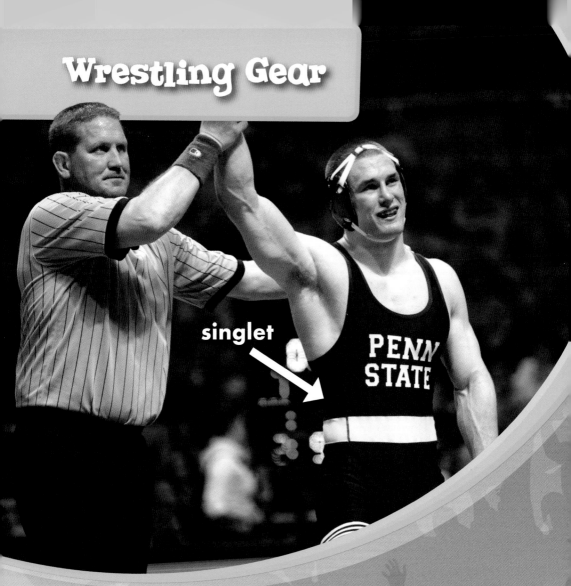

singlet

Wrestlers wear tight **singlets** during matches.

It is against the rules to grab clothing. Tight singlets make grabbing clothing **difficult**.

Safety is important. **Headgear** saves wrestlers' ears from injury. Knee pads keep wrestlers safe during falls.

headgear

knee pads

singlet

shoes

knee pads

headgear

mouth guard

Mouth guards keep their teeth safe.

Shoes are lightweight.
They have high tops
to keep ankles safe.

Two wrestlers step
onto the mat. But only
one steps away as
the winner!

# Glossary

**difficult**—hard to do

**headgear**—a guard worn over the ears to keep wrestlers safe

**holds**—wrestling moves that take control away from an opponent; holds make it difficult for an opponent to move.

**matches**—games between two individuals or teams

**neutral**—a type of position in which both wrestlers are standing

**Olympic**—related to the Olympic Games; the Olympic Games are worldwide summer or winter sports contests held in a different country every four years.

**opponents**—wrestlers on other teams

**periods**—specific amounts of time wrestlers wrestle; there are three periods in a wrestling match.

**pin**—to hold an opponent's shoulders to the mat

**singlets**—tight-fitting wrestling uniforms

**takedown**—a wrestling move used to bring an opponent down to the mat

**weight class**—a measurement that groups wrestlers by weight

# To Learn More

Doeden, Matt. *Combat Sports*. Mankato, Minn.: Amicus High Interest, 2016.

Rebman, Nick. *Wrestling*. Lake Elmo, Minn.: Focus Readers, 2019.

Sherman, Jill. *Gymnastics*. Minneapolis, Minn.: Bellwether Media, 2020.

## ON THE WEB

# FACTSURFER

Factsurfer.com gives you a safe, fun way to find more information.

1. Go to www.factsurfer.com.

2. Enter "wrestling" into the search box and click 🔍.

3. Select your book cover to see a list of related web sites.

# Index